When the Sun Doesn't Rise is an honest, open, and real account of the rollercoaster of emotions a person experiences during a prolonged period of childlessness, all the while holding onto hope and faith in God. Christina takes readers not only into the heart-wrenching journey of confronting pain, sadness, and disappointment but into the reality of trusting in the promises of our good heavenly Father and believing for His best timing and outcomes for our lives. Christina's living faith, patience, and trust is inspiring for those who find themselves in a similar position of believing God for a child. This book is also recommended for anyone who through faith and patience is still waiting to inherit their own promise from God.

—Kate Smith
Co-President, Catch the Fire World
www.catchthefire.com

When the Sun

THE

DOESN'T RISE

Installments of Faith

CHRISTINA RICHARDS

Scriptures taken from the Holy Bible, New International Version®, NIV®. Copyright © 1973, 1978, 1984, 2011 by Biblica, Inc.™ Used by permission of Zondervan. All rights reserved worldwide. www.zondervan.com The "NIV" and "New International Version" are trademarks registered in the United States Patent and Trademark Office by Biblica, Inc.™

ISBN: 978-1-4866-2673-1
eBook ISBN: 978-1-4866-2674-8

Word Alive Press
119 De Baets Street Winnipeg, MB R2J 3R9
www.wordalivepress.ca

WORD ALIVE
—P R E S S—

Cataloguing in Publication information can be obtained from Library and Archives Canada.

For God,
who gave me the idea
and then would not let me walk away.

Contents

Introduction
FAITH IN INSTALLMENTS

*Now faith is confidence in what we hope for and
assurance about what we do not see.*
(Hebrews 11:1)

I'VE HAD A great life. I grew up sheltered from the ugliness and pain that life can sometimes bring. I grew up in small-town Newfoundland where everyone knows everyone, at a time when no one locked their doors—and no one needed to. I have wonderful parents who raised me in a Christian home filled with love and affection. I have a loving husband, great friends, and a good job.

As a child, and into adulthood, I've been insulated from the pain of illness and death. My parents had moved to Newfoundland from England before I was born, so my parents, brother, and sister were the only close family I had and we were all healthy and happy. My grandparents died either when I was too young to have known them or after having lived full, happy lives.

I met my husband when I was eighteen. It was our first semester in university and five years later we were married. I got a job straight out of university and we moved to Calgary, Alberta for employment. We were blessed in many ways—new friends, jobs we enjoyed, and a comfortable home.

The only scar on an otherwise great life was the death of my aunt when I was twenty-two years old.

My Auntie Ann was a wonderful woman. She lived in England and I lived in Newfoundland, so we saw each other only occasionally, but she had a big impact on my life. Auntie Ann was an incredibly caring woman. She was always ready to help anyone in any situation. She had a great sense of humour and could be counted on to be the life of any party. You never walked away from an encounter with Auntie Ann without a smile on your face.

It can't be said about too many people, but Auntie Ann was genuine. What you saw was definitely what you got, although it's hard to believe that someone you hardly know could care so much about you. She was so full of love that it exploded out of her onto everyone around her.

When she died, the local newspaper received so many comments about her that they became interested in discovering more about her. In the end, they wrote an article about her entitled "The Woman with a Heart of Gold." She touched everyone's lives and we were all better for it. She was, in my eyes, God's hand extended.

In 1999, Auntie Ann was diagnosed with lymphatic cancer. In the summer of 2000, I visited her home in England at a time when she was undergoing chemotherapy. She was tired and not well, but her spirit hadn't changed. She wasn't focussed on herself and her situation but on those around her. She used her frequent hospital visits to minister to other patients. In true Auntie Ann style, she encouraged and listened to the plights of others. She made them smile in the midst of their pain. She loved them.

Auntie Ann was a woman of strong faith. In every situation, she firmly believed in prayer and the power of God. Her belief never wavered. She prayed, her family prayed, and people she'd impacted around the world lifted her up in prayer for healing.

After this short visit, I returned home confident that I would see her again when I visited in December. It never occurred to me that Auntie Ann would battle with cancer for the rest of the year, and it certainly never occurred to me that she would lose that battle—just two days before I arrived back in England for Christmas.

My last memory is of her sitting in her garden, surrounded by family, laughing.

Life moved on, as it always does. I graduated university, got married, and moved away. But I often thought of Auntie Ann. To me, she was an example of how life should be, of how God wants us to live—one day at a time and pouring out God's love to others. I strive to follow that example. I want to remember her by being like her.

One question, however, continued to plague me as time passed. It crept in when I least expected it and hung in the back of my mind. It's an age-old question that has been asked countless times by countless people: how could such a bad thing happen to such a good person?

For me, it was an even more specific question: how could God not heal someone with such faith? If Auntie Ann didn't have enough faith to be healed, where was the hope for the rest of us? I believed that God *could* heal. I had seen God heal. But in light of the reality I saw, how are we to have faith to pray and wholeheartedly believe that God *will* heal?

I wanted faith. I wanted to be able to pray for something and believe God would answer. I wanted to believe wholeheartedly.

I began to pursue this question. I asked other Christians, I read my Bible, I prayed to God, and I spent a lot of time thinking and praying about it.

Be careful what you pray for. God answers prayers, but He doesn't always answer them in the way we expect. I had no idea how a prayer for faith would completely change my life.

The next chapter of my life would take my great little life and turn it upside-down. God would answer my prayer, but He gave me what I needed, not necessarily what I wanted.

And He only answered my prayer in His time.

Faith is an interesting thing. It's so simple, yet also so hard to grasp, intricately linked with so many other Christian values. Learning how to have faith means learning about love, trust, peace, patience, and many other virtues at the same time.

My journey to faith wasn't a straight path but rather a winding, convoluted, often mystifying road with many pitstops along the way.

I am an organizer at heart. I inherited that trait from my mother.

I like lists. In fact, I excel at lists. I have lists for everything. My husband tells me that I talk in lists… so it makes sense that my journey to find faith came in steps—or rather, what I call install-ments. I learned one small lesson at a time, fully absorbing it before moving on to the next.

Apparently I'm a slow learner, though, because some of these lessons took me a long time to learn. God had many lessons to teach me and I went through many life-altering experiences. I prefer to view my life as a set of circumstances He has used to teach me to trust, have faith, and rest fully and completely in His perfect love.

Some people learn more easily than others. For some, learning new things comes naturally. For others, it slowly builds over time through many days of trials, sorrow, and fear.

I think my experience with Auntie Ann's death scarred me more than I realized and made my journey to faith longer and more difficult than I ever expected. My mother says that my journey has been a little like the biblical story of Job.

My co-workers, on the other hand, tell me that I have a black cloud that follows me around.

This journey toward faith has occurred over the last fifteen years, and I know that I'm still not done. But I've come a long way. I've learned that faith and trust go hand in hand. I've learned that I haven't always seen the big picture. I've learned that God never makes promises He doesn't keep. I've learned that God is in control. I've learned that God knows what I need.

Most importantly, I've learned that God loves me and wants what is best for me.

The story to follow will provide you just a glimpse into my life, including my fear of cancer and the heartache of infertility. I firmly believe that God wanted me to write this story and I hope that you learn as much from reading this as I've learned in writing it.

First Installment

GOD ANSWERS PRAYER (SOMETIMES THE ANSWER IS YES)

*Ask and it will be given to you; seek and you will
find; knock and the door will be opened to you.*
(Matthew 7:7)

MY STORY ACTUALLY begins in 2006, but I didn't know it at the time. Since I would like to take you on the same journey I took, let's fast-forward a little to October 2007.

It was fall and we had just recently moved into a new home in Calgary. My husband Deon and I had been doing some extremely physical yardwork over the Thanksgiving weekend: installing in-ground sprinklers, which involved dragging a very heavy trenching machine through the dirt. At the end of the weekend, we were exhausted and aching.

One night shortly after, I discovered a lump in my leg about the size of a golf ball. I thought it was a knotted muscle from all the hard work and assumed it would go away within a few days.

It didn't go away, so a few weeks later I made an appointment with my doctor to get it checked out.

My appointment came in early December. The doctor examined my leg and suggested that I get an ultrasound. By this time, the lump was now the size of a small apple.

Since the doctor seemed concerned, I left for an immediate ultrasound before going on vacation to Newfoundland for Christmas. At the doctor's request, I left my contact information.

1

Just three days before Christmas, I was shocked when I received a call to inform me that the ultrasound was inconclusive. I was being referred to a specialist. When could I come in for another appointment?

I scheduled that appointment to take place right after my return to Calgary.

When I saw the specialist, he immediately ruled out certain causes and sent me for a biopsy. Within a week, I had completed the biopsy.

Because this test was also inconclusive, next I was sent for an MRI.

I went from doctor to doctor, test to test. Looking back, one of the scariest aspects of the whole experience was how quickly everything moved. My experience with the medical field to date had been that everything took a long time. I had learned that if the doctors were concerned enough, things could move really fast. So the faster they moved, the scarier the situation got.

Finally, in February 2008, the diagnosis was in: sarcoma, cancer of the muscle tissue. The treatment plan was to include chemotherapy, followed by radiation, followed by surgery. It would be an aggressive treatment, but by this time the lump was the size of my fist.

We cancelled our upcoming vacation, a Caribbean cruise, and I arranged to take time off work.

Cancer has to be one of the scariest words in the English language. Most people know of someone whose life has been altered by cancer—but unless you've experienced it personally, it's difficult to comprehend just how devastating it can be to hear those words—"You have cancer"—from the doctor's mouth.

Cancer. These six little letters will turn your life upside-down.

My family was devastated. Deon was angry. I was numb. I had prayed for faith, and this certainly required faith, but I found that I wasn't up to the task. I couldn't bring myself to ask God for healing.

So instead I asked God for help in handling what was to come. I knew God *could* heal... but what if He didn't heal me?

Feeling afraid, I leaned heavily on the prayers of my family and friends. I added my name to the prayer list at my church. People from across the country and other countries were praying for me.

But on a personal level, I prepared to battle the same disease that had claimed my aunt's life. I would go through the treatments. I could do this. I would fight. I would win.

It's always amazing to me how God uses the people you least expect to impact your life in significant ways. In my case, there was Ada, a little elderly lady at my church who I didn't know very well but often saw worshipping excitedly on Sunday mornings. She was a sight to behold, dancing and clapping along with old hymns and new choruses alike. She was a woman secure in the knowledge that God was her rock and salvation.

A mutual friend asked me whether she could get Ada to pray for me. I agreed, and one Sunday morning I met with both of them before church.

Ada prayed for me. To this day, I don't remember her words, but I do remember her faith. She prayed for healing. Complete healing. She went directly into the throne room of God and talked to Him about me. She didn't ask that I would survive the treatments or that He would use the doctors and medication to make me better; she prayed that the cancer would be completely gone. Just disappear. A complete healing. I was amazed at her confidence but could not find that faith within myself.

One week later, I sat in an examination room with my husband. We were there to find out the results of yet another test and discuss our next steps. We could hear doctors talking outside the room but couldn't understand the fragmented conversation.

The longer I waited, the more anxious I became.

Finally, my doctor came into the examination room with two other doctors I had never seen before. I felt nervous. But as we sat there, speechless, the three doctors told us that they were "confounded" by the results of my most recent biopsy. In fact, they were so confused that they had requested that the test results be re-examined. They had even gone so far as to take my case to the hospital's board for consultation.

They couldn't explain it, but the cancer wasn't there anymore. I could explain it, though. I was healed. Somebody had faith and I was healed.

Mark 5 gives us the story of the woman with the issue of blood. In fact, this story is also recorded in Matthew 9 and Luke 8. This woman had been sick for twelve years. Every time I read this story, I think, *I can barely manage to deal with the flu for a week.* Twelve years is a really long time to be sick, so she had to be desperate. Just imagine the heartache that she must have suffered. She must have tried everything to get better.

The Bible doesn't tell us, but we can imagine that she paid multiple visits to doctors, enduring expensive, painful, or embarrassing treatments. Potentially she was shunned by friends and family.

The Bible does tell us that nothing she did worked. She must have felt incredibly discouraged.

But then she heard about Jesus. She picked herself up again and went for healing. This time, if she could just touch the hem of His robe, she would be healed.

She pressed in, pushed her way through the crowd, then reached out and just barely touched Jesus's robe. We don't know if she received an instant healing or whether she felt it slowly flow through her body, but we do know that Jesus noticed. He felt the healing power leave him.

Upon discovering who had touched Him, He said, *"Your faith has healed you"* (Matthew 9:22, Mark 5:34, Luke 8:48).

She believed. Jesus healed.

It sounds so simple: just believe and God will heal. It worked for me too. Somebody believed and I was healed.

As you can imagine, my family and I were overjoyed. But inside? Well, I was experiencing a bit of disbelief. I left the hospital and stood in the parking lot with Deon. We just stood there, speechlessly holding each other as we waited for the truth to sink in.

I was healed. The cancer was gone.

God had healed me because someone asked. Ever since I was a little child, I had heard the words of Matthew 7:7 repeated over and over: *"Ask and it will be given to you..."* It couldn't be that simple, could it?

My first installment of faith came from hearing someone else's prayer.

Just ask. Just believe. Sometimes the answer is yes!

Second Installment
HIS EYE IS ON THE SPARROW

Are not two sparrows sold for a penny? Yet not
one of them will fall to the ground outside your
Father's care. And even the very hairs of your
head are all numbered. So don't be afraid; you
are worth more than many sparrows.
(Matthew 10:29–31)

THE YEAR 2008 was a particularly difficult year for me and Deon. Healed from cancer in February, I never dreamed that by the end of the year I would have been protected not once, but twice, more from life-threatening events.

Let me set the scene. It's May and summer has arrived early in Calgary. After my brush with cancer and our cancelled Caribbean vacation, Deon and I decided that a weekend away was just what we needed to relax and renew ourselves.

Deon had a brand-new motorcycle and we decided to use the May long weekend to take a three-day trip to Medicine Hat. As we drove out onto the highway and left the city behind, we enjoyed the beautiful sunshine and unseasonably warm weather. It was a perfect weekend for a motorbike trip, with nothing but open road in front of us.

We were about ten minutes outside Calgary, travelling at about 110 kilometres per hour, when the unthinkable happened. A woman drove her minivan through a stop sign and crossed the road

7

right in front of us. Deon slammed on the brakes and tried to stop, but it was too late. We were too close. We hit the back end of her vehicle with a sickening crunch and popped the bike's front tire. The bike fell onto its side and slid through the intersection… with Deon and me tumbling along the road behind it.

I don't actually remember the details of the accident. I hit my head on the road and briefly lost consciousness as I tumbled from the motorbike. I know that I screamed and for days afterwards Deon would wake up in the middle of the night reliving that sound. I remember standing in the middle of the road immediately after the accident, thinking to myself that I needed to get off the road. I remember wondering how the pickup truck that had been behind us could now be in front of us without having hit us.

Miraculously, we were relatively unhurt. We didn't go to the hospital at the time.

But when the adrenaline wore off later that night, we made our way to the emergency room where I was treated for a slight concussion and Deon for a dislocated thumb. The whiplash I suffered in my lower back would go on to cause back pain for years to come, but we were alive and walking. A few seconds different and it would have been a completely different story.

God is a God of miracles. We were alive.

Let's fast-forward a few months to December of the same year. It was an emotionally rough Christmas for me, the first time we weren't spending it with either of our families. We were by ourselves in Calgary while my family was at my sister's house in Ontario. We'd been unable to make the trip to Ontario due to work commitments.

I was feeling pretty low, so Deon and I decided to take a Sunday drive and spend the afternoon in Banff. It was a beautiful day and warm for December, but the temperature hovered right around the freezing point. As we got closer to the mountains, the water on the roads began to freeze.

We hit a patch of black ice and lost control of our vehicle. We flew off the road at about 110 kilometres per hour. Our vehicle flipped three to four times before coming to a stop.

People always say that accidents happen so fast that you don't have time to react. That's true in one sense. But when it's happening, it also feels like slow motion. I recall my head hitting the side panel each time the vehicle rolled over. I also remember Deon repeatedly asking me whether I was okay.

In the end, the vehicle landed on the shoulder of the other side of the divided highway, with oncoming traffic coming to a standstill. Deon had to stand on the driver's side window and hold me up to release my seatbelt. Then we pushed open the passenger door and climbed out.

The driver who had stopped to help later told me that he'd seen the accident happen as our vehicle hurtled towards him. His first thought had been that there was no way anyone would survive the accident. Again, miraculously, we walked away alive and well with only a few minor cuts and scratches and another bout of whiplash.

God is a God of miracles. We were alive.

Both accidents caused me to thank God for His protection. Either accident could have been much worse if the situation had been slightly different. I recognized that we had been protected.

Looking back, I can see that I was receiving another install-ment in my faith journey. God often protects us from things we couldn't even begin to predict or imagine.

Let me put it this way. God cares about me. God has a plan for me. Like a sparrow, His eye is on me and my life. Sometimes He gives me what I ask for, but other times He takes care of me without me needing to ask. He loves me that much.

Third Installment
WANTING WHAT GOD WANTS

This is the confidence we have in approaching
God: that if we ask anything according
to his will, he hears us.
(1 John 5:14)

THIS STORY ISN'T necessarily told in chronological order—unusual for me, since I tend to think in logical, organized lists!—so allow me to skip back in time to 2001. I was twenty-three years old and had just gotten married, finished university, and started a new job.

And much to my surprise, I was beginning to realize that I had a desire to have a baby.

Now, that may not sound like a surprise, considering that I was a young married woman. But I had never really thought much about children before this. Although I guess I always expected to have kids, I definitely wasn't one of those girls who dreamt of being a mother. Given that I was young, newly married, and just starting my career, I had pushed that idea into the background, something to do "later."

Looking back, I believe that God was planting a seed of desire.

That "later" came in 2006—and yes, I have now come forward in time to the point where my faith journey began. My husband and I decided we were the perfect age to begin a family. I had spent five years putting my career first and getting a foothold in my chosen field. Now I was ready to concentrate on having a family. I was excited and allowed my imagination to run wild with plans and ideas.

In August of that year, I stopped taking my birth control pills and expected that within a few months God would bless us with a child.

It sounded so simple. I never imagined it wouldn't happen. After all, women have been getting pregnant since Adam and Eve. I didn't even know any women who hadn't been able to have children. I had no frame of reference for any other scenario.

Expectation turned to disappointment when I was diagnosed with polycystic ovary syndrome and told that getting pregnant would be a little more difficult than expected. Although we were told it certainly wasn't impossible, we would need to be proactive. My family doctor referred me to the fertility clinic in Calgary, as a precaution. From there, I began a variety of treatments that extended through the next few years, interrupted only by cancer treatments and the lingering effects of multiple motor vehicle accidents. Apparently it's difficult to get pregnant when you put so much stress on your body!

To fully appreciate the lessons I've learned, I should interject here by including a bit of history. I have recently recognized that I am a bit of a control freak. That term usually comes with negative connotations, but there are many positive aspects to this trait as well. The plusses revolve around being organized, accomplishing tasks, and getting things done. I do well in my chosen field of employment as it requires me to take charge, make sense of chaos, and meet targets.

The downside, of course, is that I like to be in charge. I "know" how best to get things done and want others to do things my way. While this is an asset in my job, it creates many problems in my relationship with God and my ability to have faith in Him.

The next big lesson God had for me is that *my* way is not *His* way. We can only truly pray with confidence that He will answer our prayer if we pray in union with His will.

Let me explain that a little further. Think back to when you were a child and really wanted something—for example, a chocolate bar before supper or to stay at a friend's house overnight. When you asked your parents, you likely got one of a few possible responses. If you asked for a chocolate bar before supper, you probably were told, "No, it's too close to supper and not good for you." Your parent, knowing better than you, was looking out for your best interests. If you asked to stay at a friend's house overnight, you may have been told, "Yes." Again, your parent was able to see that this would make you happy and allowing it wouldn't cause any problems or concerns.

Now think about how *you* would have felt when you asked for these things. In each scenario, you probably knew what the answer would be before you asked. Asking for something when you knew your parents would agree would have been easy. Asking for something when you weren't sure is more difficult.

Praying in faith is essentially the same principle. It's easy for us to pray in faith when we know that we're asking for something God wants for us. It's difficult to pray in faith when we don't know whether our request is in line with His plan.

13

Back to my story. In 2008 and 2009, we attended many appointments at the fertility clinic. The first step was to be tested. We very quickly learned that there was nothing wrong with either of us. There was no specific problem and everything worked the way it should. Except I couldn't seem to get pregnant.

The next step involved being prescribed medication to speed up the process. This medication had several unfortunate side effects, triggering many common symptoms of pregnancy. The biggest impact on my daily life, and my husband's, was the hormone-induced emotional rollercoaster. I was constantly on the verge of tears. Any little thing could send me into hysterics beyond my control. The funny thing was, I knew when I was being emotional and unreasonable; I just couldn't seem to stop it.

For example, while drying and putting away some dishes one day, I ran into a problem with my pot drawer. Pot drawers are wonderful, but my pot drawer is a little crowded and requires a specific placement in order for everything to fit. On this particular day, I was trying to take shortcut and *make* everything fit. As you can imagine, things didn't go my way. Within moments, I let out a cry of frustration and crumpled to the floor in a tearful mess.

This is how my husband found me when he came running down the stairs to check whether I was hurt. To his credit, he just bundled me up in his arms and held me until the tears stopped.

After months and many cycles of hope and despair, it became obvious that the medication wasn't helping the way it should. So my doctor advised us to move to the next step: intrauterine insemination (IUI).

Anybody who has struggled with infertility and gone through this process can tell you that it takes all the intimacy out of making a baby and transforms it into something mechanical, programmed, and sterile. Trying to conceive is intensely personal, intimate, and emotional, but IUI is all about tests, labs, and doctors.

Nevertheless, we pushed forward and completed three cycles of IUI—but to no avail. I still wasn't pregnant.

By early 2009, my husband and I had tried everything but invitro fertilization. Nothing had worked and I was still childless in my thirties. I once again faced an unwelcome diagnosis, this time "unexplained infertility."

Anyone who has been through the pain of infertility knows the emotional rollercoaster that accompanies it. My emotions bounced around like I was the ball inside a pinball machine. One week I would be hopeful; the next week I'd be in utter despair. I was angry, sad, desperate, and obsessed. I would cry myself to sleep.

My life began to revolve around my obsessive desire to have children. I couldn't let it go, and I certainly couldn't leave it in God's hands.

So I prayed… a lot. I begged and pleaded with God. But each morning, I would pick up my burden again and carry it around with me.

I tried everything in my control to get pregnant and nothing worked. But instead of giving my burden to God, I deluded myself into thinking that I could solve the problem myself. I thought that God was trying to teach me something. If I could just figure it out, He would answer my prayer.

Even as I write this, I know that words will never adequately describe how I really felt. I began to wonder whether I was depressed. I felt like crying all the time. My emotions were so close to the surface that I thought everyone must be able to see what was going on.

Up to this point, we hadn't told anyone that we were trying to have a child, so I had no one with whom to share my pain except my husband. He, of course, was going through his own kind of pain. I wanted to be strong for him and stay positive, but it was an act. Inside, I was falling apart.

Adding to our pain and frustration was the constant barrage of questions from family, friends, and even casual acquaintances.

"When are you having kids?"

"Do you know you're not getting any younger?"

"When are you going to give us grandkids/nieces/nephews/cousins?"

Each question was well-intentioned, but they still cut deep.

One particularly painful incident came at the hands of a co-worker. Now a mother of two, she had experienced fertility issues herself and felt like she had experience. She wanted to help.

Around my thirtieth birthday, I came to work one morning to find a printout of an internet article on my desk. The article was entitled "Making Time for Baby" and was all about how career women wait too long to have children. My co-worker felt it was important for me to know that studies showed that fertility in women decreased after age twenty-seven, so I shouldn't put off having kids any longer.

She had even highlighted sections of the article that she felt were particularly important. I closed my office door and cried my eyes out.

Right around this time, a book by Paul Young called *The Shack* was hitting the bestseller lists. The book tells the story of a father whose daughter has died. He feels compelled to visit a shack where he meets with God, Jesus, and the Holy Spirit.

In one scene, the author describes an encounter with Jesus in the garden. When the father arrives, the garden is a mess of weeds—but during the conversation, almost without notice, Jesus transforms the garden into something beautiful. The underlying theme of this scene is that our lives are a mess. Whether we've messed it up or something has happened to mess it up, we are living in a mess. Jesus can use that mess and transform it into something beautiful. It doesn't matter who we are, where we are, or how much we have messed things up in our attempt to "control" our lives; Jesus can make it beautiful. We just have to let Him.

This message was driven home in January 2009 when Deon and I went to a concert in Edmonton for the Christian band Mercy Me. During the show, the lead singer said something that spoke right to my heart, and it's stuck with me ever since. He was talking about the death of his father and how he had been unable to make sense of why such a good man had died at a time when he needed him the most.

"We are so close to what is happening in our own lives that things often don't seem to make sense, but God can see the big picture," he said. "He has all the pieces laid out in the palm of His hand. I believe that God is up in heaven looking down at our lives, saying, 'Just you wait. What I've got in store for you is going to blow your mind!'"

That's when I received my third installment of faith. In a flash of understanding, I realized that my plans were not the same as the plans God had for me. I was trying to put the puzzle together the way I wanted it to go, but I was unable to see all the pieces. God showed me that I needed to accept that I don't have all the answers and recognize that He does.

God knows what He's doing. He knows us. In fact, He knew us in our mothers' wombs (Jeremiah 1:5). He also knows what He wants for us, having great plans for our lives (Jeremiah 29:11). My job was simple: I must accept it.

It was also around this time that my doctor at the fertility clinic informed us that our next (and final) option was invitro fertilization (IVF). Deon and I had discussed this option. While Deon's mind was made up on the issue, I was still in a state of confusion. Our friends and family had seen both success and failure using IVF. Deon felt very strongly that we shouldn't take this route.

I took this to God in prayer and eventually realized that my reluctance to give up on the IVF option was another attempt for me to control the situation. God didn't need to use IVF for me to get pregnant. He is a God of miracles.

Many people would argue that God can use different methods to answer prayer, and I believe that with all my heart, but I felt that He was asking me to accept His plan. If it was His plan for me to get pregnant, I didn't need IVF to do that. If it was His plan for me not to get pregnant, there was no reason to go ahead with IVF anyway.

We decided to not go ahead with IVF and my time at the fertility clinic came to an end.

I needed to accept that God's plan was different than mine. But if I accepted that, where would I go from here? Instead of being frustrated that my plan wasn't working, I found myself in limbo. If my plan was not God's plan... then what was God's plan? How could I begin to accept His plan if I didn't know what it was?

In hindsight, I wonder why I didn't let go of my control issues earlier. When my life was spinning out of control, I kept trying to hang on. My version of acceptance was waiting for God to do what I wanted Him to do.

In mid-2009, I reached my lowest point. As often happens when we reach our lowest point, I gave up trying to handle things on my own and cried out to God. I recognized that I could no longer handle the pain.

I remember very clearly the moment I cried out to God in desperation. I was walking home from the bus stop after work and praying, as I often did. I simultaneously asked God for His will and begged Him to allow me to have a child.

At some point, in the midst of my pain, I said, "If it's not your will for me to have children, take the desire away!"

This was a short sentence, but it meant something *big*. This gut-wrenching prayer was the turning point in my journey. I had handed *my* plans over to God and asked that He replace them with *His* plans. It was incredibly liberating to realize that the only requirement being asked of me was to allow God to give me the desire of His heart. I just had to accept it, sit back, and let Him do the rest.

Do you remember how carefree you were as a child? Your parents had all the responsibility and did all the planning. You just had to go where you were told and do what you were told.

As a child, our family went on a vacation to England. My parents, of course, planned everything. I just went along, happily enjoying what life had to offer. This isn't to say I didn't have choices. I did. But I didn't have to worry about the details. I could just get up in the morning, enjoy the day, and rely on Mom and Dad to ensure that I got where I was going, had food to eat, and had a bed to sleep in.

Somewhere along the way of growing up and taking on adult responsibilities, we lose that sense of freedom and learn how to worry. God was telling me that I needed to be more like a child and depend one hundred percent on Him. I needed to accept that I was His child.

It didn't happen overnight. But once I learned to accept God's plan and start releasing my control issues, He filled me with an incredible peace. I felt a huge weight being lifted off my shoulders.

Indeed it had. I was no longer solely responsible for my future.

I won't say that there weren't days when I reverted back to my old self. That would be a lie. There have been many days since when I've had to remind myself that God's plan is perfect. Since that first breakthrough, I have prayed the same prayer over and over again: "God, if this desire isn't from You, please take it away." It doesn't always come easy, but it does come with a tremendous reward—peace.

Fourth Installment

GOD ANSWERS PRAYER (SOMETIMES THE ANSWER IS WAIT!)

> *For I am the Lord your God who takes hold of*
> *your right hand and says to you,*
> *Do not fear; I will help you.*
> (Isaiah 41:13)

OBVIOUSLY THIS IS not where my story ends. Although I prayed for God to take away my desire for a child if it wasn't His plan, He didn't. My desire to have a child never wavered. I now felt confident that it was in God's plan for me to have a child. I was praying in accordance with God's will...

But I still wasn't getting pregnant.

The same passage in Mark 5 that describes the woman with the issue of blood and her immediate healing upon touching Jesus's garment tells another story, this one about a man named Jairus.

Jairus's daughter was sick, so he came looking for Jesus to heal her. He knew that if Jesus came to see his daughter, she would be okay. When Jesus agreed, they left to visit the man's home—but along the way, Jesus was detained. While Jairus waited for Jesus to finish, he received word that his daughter had died.

We aren't told how long Jairus had been waiting. When I first read this story, I assumed it was just a short period. But what if it was longer than that? What if Jairus had been made to wait for days? Any parent can imagine how excruciating it would be to wait while their child is sick.

In the end, Jairus told Jesus not to bother coming to his house anymore since his daughter had already died.

Jesus insisted on going anyway. When they got to the house, Jesus went in, saw the girl, and declared, *"The child is not dead but asleep"* (Mark 5:39). That's when Jesus raised the girl from the dead and reunited her with her father. Jairus had to wait, but God answered his prayer.

The Bible contains many examples of women enduring infertility and a season of waiting before God answered their prayers for a child. One of the most well-known stories is of Sarah, who waited more than twenty-five years for Isaac to be born. Rebekah waited nearly as long, twenty years, for her son Jacob. Rachel, Elizabeth, and Hannah all suffered from infertility, prayed fervently for God to heal them, and spent long periods of time waiting for God to answer their prayer.

Knowing this doesn't take away the pain and frustration of waiting, but it does give me a hopeful reminder that God has proven Himself faithful to deliver time after time.

I read a lot of books, particularly romances, and am very familiar with the trope of the story's heroine having to wait for her happy ending. The problem with books is that these happy endings need to happen within a few hundred pages. It seems to me that the characters never have to wait for years for their prayers to be answered.

I struggled with this for a long while—until God chose to speak to me not once, but twice, telling me that I needed to wait.

The first time God spoke to me about waiting, I was walking from one office building to another during my workday. My company had recently merged with another and my time was often split between two offices. I spent a lot of time walking back and forth and often passed pregnant women. There seemed to be a baby boom in Calgary!

On this particular day, I passed a woman who was obviously quite far along in her pregnancy. I was immediately hit with a pang of longing.

I know You have a plan, God, and I'm trying to be patient, I prayed. *But I need something from You. I need to know that Your answer is "Wait," not "No."*

God suddenly placed words within my heart—not audible, but nonetheless very real and unmistakable: *"Fear not. Your time is coming soon."*

I believe that God speaks to us. My experience has been that usually he speaks to me through a Bible verse or sermon that resonates with me and becomes lodged in my mind and heart.

It's not very often that I hear God speak directly to me and drop words in my mind. As a result, my response to these words was to question God again. Had I just made up those words in my own head? I asked God to give me some tangible proof, something that I couldn't mistake for my own thoughts.

I didn't have to wait long.

Later that night, as I prepared to relax with a good book, I grabbed a random book out of my new stack and prepared to read. As I opened the book, I noted the scripture on the first page: *"For I am the Lord your God who takes hold of your right hand and says to you, Do not fear; I will help you"* (Isaiah 41:13).

If I'm honest, I must admit that I was stunned. In fact, I was so surprised that I stopped walking across the room and just stood there in tears. I knew that God had answered my prayer and given me a tangible sign. I was supposed to wait.

The second time God spoke to me about waiting was about six months later. I was still clinging to God's direction to wait, although I was finding it harder and harder every day.

I should back up a little to tell you about sunrises and what they mean to me. Somewhere in my past, years and years ago, I heard someone say that sunrises are the result of God painting you a picture to show how much He loves you. I have always loved that sentiment and am reminded of it every time I see a sunrise.

One morning, on my way to work on the train, I was standing near the front of the car facing the window. I don't recall anymore what had happened that morning to precipitate my frame of mind, but I remember that I was upset and talking to God—using my inside voice, so as to not scare my fellow commuters! I asked about my infertility and His plan for me.

As the train came around some buildings, I saw the most beautiful sunrise laid out before me. Before I had time to think, God placed some words in my heart. They weren't audible, but they were so clear and specific that I couldn't deny they had come from God. They came to me one line at a time. When it was finished, I was speechless and in tears.

> This sunrise is for you
> To remind you
> That I have not forgotten you

I remember My promise to you
Your time is coming soon

God was once again reiterating His message to me: I was to keep waiting. I still didn't know the details of His plan for me, but I knew that He wasn't saying no. Although I didn't know how long I would have to wait, I was thrilled to know there was a day coming when I would get to hear my child call me "Mom."

At the time, it felt like my wait was almost over. But that was not to be the case.

Many years have passed since God asked me to wait. It hasn't been easy and I haven't always been gracious in my waiting period, but God has been using that time to teach me. I have more lessons to learn.

Fifth Installment

TRUST

When I am afraid, I put my trust in you.
(Psalm 56:3)

WHILE READING THE Christmas story in the first chapter of Matthew, as I do every year, I was struck by how much trust Mary and Joseph must have had.

Mary trusted in God enough to accept an unexpected and "impossible" pregnancy, knowing that it would completely change her life in ways she couldn't control. Joseph trusted in God enough to take his wife despite cultural convention and logic. His friends and family must have thought he was completely crazy.

Together, as a family, Mary and Joseph trusted God enough to pack up in the middle of the night and head for Egypt.

My husband and I packed up and moved to Alberta for work knowing where we were going, what we would do when we got here, and that a quick plane trip would get us back home in less than a day. It was still incredibly scary and nerve-wracking.

Mary and Joseph didn't know where they were going, what they would do when they got there, or whether they would ever see their home again. And two years later, they trusted God enough to pack up yet again and move back to a home where the king had wanted to kill their son.

These aren't small decisions resulting in small changes. These are monumental, life-altering decisions that we now know had ramifications for the next two thousand years and beyond.

Yet Mary and Joseph put their trust in God and He delivered on His promises.

Faith and trust go hand in hand. If you don't trust God, how do you have faith to believe that He will answer your prayer? This was to be my next lesson.

For my part, I thought I had this one nailed. I trusted God. Of course I did. After all, I had been a Christian since I was a child. I could look back over my life and see the points at which I had trusted God for something big.

When I was twenty years old, I trusted God when He told me to go on a short-term missions trip to Haiti. I was a poor student at the time, saddled with loans, and yet God had told me to go and I made the decision to trust His provision. I hadn't known where the money would come from.

At the time, I had a promise box with individual little cards with Bible verses on them. I finished praying one day and randomly chose a promise card. I was shocked to read a verse from Exodus which said, *"And the Lord said to Moses "Go..."* (Exodus 19:10) The very next day, I made the commitment to go to Haiti—and God provided the funds in time for the deadline. My life was forever changed on that trip as I interacted with children from one of the poorest countries in the world.

When I was twenty-three years old, I moved away from home to build a new life in a strange place. My new husband and I hadn't wanted to leave the only home we had ever known to start anew

We are Newfoundland, born and bred, and the idea of moving away hadn't sat very well with us. But we'd felt that God was asking us to do this, so we trusted Him, packed up, and moved. God provided good jobs, great friends, and a wonderful home on the other side of the country.

I could go on telling stories of those times when I chose to trust God's direction. As I look back, I can see how trusting in Him has shaped my life.

I soon found out, though, that I did not have this lesson nailed. It turned out that my previous experiences had been relatively easy compared to what God now had in store for me.

If God had told me that I would have to wait more than a decade for a child, I think I would have been able to handle it. That's a long time to wait, but at least I would have known there was a light at the end of the tunnel.

Unfortunately for me, God chose not to reveal His plans to me. So every month I would get my hopes up only to be disappointed again.

After many repetitions of this cycle, I started to take subconscious measures to protect myself from the pain and disappointment. It's human nature to shy away from the things that continue to cause us pain. I found myself talking less and less with God. My prayer life became stilted and I felt far away from Him.

Trust is a decision. We make daily decisions to trust based on our experiences. We easily trust people who have proven themselves and struggle to trust those who have let us down time and time again.

Although I had trusted God in the past and He had proven trustworthy in those matters, nothing I had encountered before had been as big or as close to my heart as wanting a child. I began to recognize in myself that I was waiting for God to answer my prayer. Until He did, I was protecting myself from further pain by not asking for anything else.

Once I recognized this behaviour, I had to learn to work through it.

Month after month, year after year, I have made almost daily decisions to trust God and let the pain go. Trust has been the longest lesson for me to learn. I struggle to trust that God knows what He is doing. I have periods when I think I've finally learned to trust Him only to have those same doubts creep back in.

I've learned not to focus on what I don't have but consciously put that aside and focus on the future. I've learned that lesson over and over.

Trust is a decision—but by making that decision often enough, it becomes a little easier and a little easier. I apply that decision to trust to all aspects my life now, not just regarding my desire for children.

I listen to a lot of music, and it seems like every year or so a new song comes along that speaks to my heart and becomes my mantra. In 2015, almost ten years into my faith journey, I heard a song by Lauren Daigle that talks about crying out to God and trusting Him when He doesn't move the mountains we want moved or answer the questions we want answered.

These words perfectly describe the journey God has put me through, and walked with me through. Like the woman with the issue of blood, He could have answered my prayer instantly. He chose instead to allow me to walk through this journey with Him and teach me to trust Him. This definitely isn't the journey I would have chosen for myself. But as I look back, I can see the good work He has done in me.

Sixth Installment

LOVE

Jesus loves me, this I know, for the Bible tells
me so. Little ones to him belong;
they are weak, but he is strong.[1]
—Anna Bartlett Warner

LOVE AND TRUST often go hand in hand. It's very difficult to love someone you don't trust. It can also be very difficult to trust someone who you don't love or who doesn't love you.

God's next lesson for me was that He loves me—and because He loves me, He doesn't want to hurt me. Therefore, I can trust Him to keep His promise to me.

As I've mentioned, I grew up in a Christian home having known Jesus all my life. I sang "Jesus Loves Me" a million times as a child. I knew God loved me. I've experienced His many blessings in my life.

While I knew this in my head, my heart never truly understood the depths of God's love.

Unlike some of the other lessons I've learned, realizing the truth and the depths of God's love for me came slowly. It didn't come as a flash of understanding but gradually seeped into my heart and mind over a longer period of time.

---

[1] Anna Bartlett Warner, "Jesus Loves Me, This I Know," 1859.

Understanding God's love for me came through praying and reading the Bible and spending time thinking about how far He had already brought me in my journey.

In my personal devotions one morning, I remember reading from Ephesians. Many prayers in this book really spoke to me, but none more than Ephesians 3:17–19:

> ...so that Christ may dwell in your hearts through faith. And I pray that you, being rooted and established in love, may have power, together with all the Lord's holy people, to grasp how wide and long and high and deep is the love of Christ, and to know this love that surpasses knowledge— that you may be filled to the measure of all the fullness of God.

Several shrubs grow in the flower planter in the front of my house. Although it can get very windy in Calgary, in particular when the Chinook winds start to blow, those plants are rooted deep. Deon and I—well, Deon more than me—have watered these shrubs and cared for them for more than a decade. Every year, the roots grower deeper into the ground. The wind can blow, the rain can come, and flowers may be knocked off, but the plant stays strong.

While reading this passage of scripture, I imagined sinking my hands deep into the soil of God's love and holding on. Trials and pain can batter me, but I'll hold on. My roots are deep in God's marvellous love. Trusting Him is like constantly watering my shrubs.

The more I trust Him, the deeper my roots go and the more I realize *"how wide and long and high and deep"* His love for me is.

The best part is that the more I realize His love for me, the more I trust Him. Because He loves me, I know He doesn't want to hurt me. Therefore, I can trust Him to keep His promise to me.

I can recount example after example of God's love for me throughout this journey. He has taught me what love looks like by blessing me with loving parents and a loving husband. He has shown that He loves me by sending a friend when I needed support or giving me strength when I felt I was about to break from the disappointment. But I have also learned to see His love for me in the beauty of the sunrise or the stillness of a summer's evening as I sit on the deck. I see it in a thousand different moments, in a thousand different ways. He has taught me to recognize and appreciate how much He loves me.

Knowing that He loves me is key to my journey of faith. If He loves me, I can trust that He will do what is best for me. If He loves me, I can be content where I am. If He loves me, I can be at peace and not need to worry. It's the foundation that supports everything else.

Yes, Jesus loves me!

.

Seventh Installment

PEACE

Do not be anxious about anything, but in
every situation, by prayer and petition, with
thanksgiving, present your requests to God.
And the peace of God, which transcends all
understanding, will guard your hearts
and your minds in Christ Jesus.
(Philippians 4:6–7)

ACCORDING TO MERRIAM-Webster, peace can be defined as "free-dom from disquieting or oppressive thoughts or emotions."[2] As many of us would agree, in the midst of our trials and storms, peace can feel elusive.

Growing up in church, I had heard all about the perfect peace of God and believed in it wholeheartedly. I read about it, sang about it, and prayed for others to have peace in their struggles. I had also experienced it in small ways. For example, in the peace that I was making a right decision, the peace that I was going where God want-ed me to go, and the peace that salvation brings, knowing that I am a child of God.

Despite this knowledge and experience, I can honestly say that I'm not sure I understood the depths of despair that could exist or how that chasm could be so completely filled by the peace God offers.

---

[2] "Peace," *Merriam-Webster.* Date of access: February 3, 2025 (https://www.merri-am-webster.com/dictionary/peace).

Ever since I was a young child in Sunday school, I have heard the story in the Mark about Jesus calming the storm. To me, that story was all about God's power to do anything. We can ask anything of God and nothing is impossible because even the storms listen when He speaks.

That's an important lesson. The story *is* about that.

But God showed me that this story is also about the peace that comes from knowing that God is in control.

> That day when evening came, he said to his disciples, "Let us go over to the other side." Leaving the crowd behind, they took him along, just as he was, in the boat. There were also other boats with him. A furious squall came up, and the waves broke over the boat, so that it was nearly swamped. Jesus was in the stern, sleeping on a cushion. The disciples woke him and said to him, "Teacher, don't you care if we drown?"
>
> He got up, rebuked the wind and said to the waves, "Quiet! Be still!" Then the wind died down and it was completely calm. (Mark 4:35–39)

Even as I looked up the definition of peace and began to write this chapter, I received fresh revelations regarding the peace God has brought into my life.

This journey started with me in turmoil. Like the storm the disciples found themselves in, my disappointments dominated my thoughts almost constantly and left me in chaos and confusion.

Whenever I allowed my mind time to wander, it inevitably wandered right back into turmoil and disappointment. Figuratively speaking, I was tossed by the winds and waves of infertility until I felt scared, alone, and vulnerable.

With the luxury of time, I can look back and see how God's peace has bit by bit calmed the storm in my heart. It didn't happen instantly, like it did for the disciples in the boat. Instead, with each passing month, I've leaned more and more into Jesus's arms. He takes away the fear and disappointment and replaces it with peace.

Perhaps the most obvious example of this is in how I've learned to handle the recurring disappointment of learning that I'm not yet pregnant. In the beginning, this news would send me into despair. There would be lots of tears accompanied by a deep-seated despair that lasted for days. During those few days, I would find it hard to pray and often took a break from spending time with God. This would be followed by days of anger as I expressed to God my frustration and lack of understanding. By the time I was coming out of this funk, the whole cycle would start again with another disappointment.

Over time, God has shown me that He can replace my pain with peace and calm the storm that rages within me.

More than a decade later, that disappointment is now immediately met with prayer: "God, please give me the strength to handle this disappointment and peace to know that Your plan is good." As I pray that prayer, I feel God saying, "Peace, be still!"

I'm not going to say that the pain goes away, because it doesn't. But it feels like God puts a lid on that pain. He contains it to one small part so that it doesn't overwhelm me. He allows me to not just survive but thrive. He gives me peace.

Eighth Installment

CONTENTMENT

> *...for I have learned to be content whatever the*
> *circumstances... I have learned the secret of*
> *being content in any and every situation... I can*
> *do all this through him who gives me strength.*
> (Philippians 4:11–13)

THERE'S AN OLD saying that tells us life is a journey, not a destination. To many people today, this is backwards. Society as a whole behaves as if life is about the destination. When we're children, we want to be grown up. When we're in high school, we want to be out on our own. Then we want to be married, have kids, and eventually retire. Our lives are measured by milestones. We set goals, but we want to achieve them instantly. And we aren't content until we've made a certain dollar amount or lost those ten pounds. We're firmly focussed on the future but fail to stop and enjoy where we are.

Somewhere along my journey, I heard a Sunday morning sermon on being content where we are. I remember the speaker, who was the wife of one our church's pastors. She spoke very genuinely about what it means to be content where you are. We might not be where we want to be, but we are where God has placed us—so we should learn to embrace it and be content.

This was especially impactful to me since she was in the middle of a tough battle with cancer.

What impressed me most was that she didn't have her eyes fixed on a future where she was healed, although she was believing in God to heal her. Her eyes were firmly fixed on where she was and learning to be content through the journey. I was amazed by her ability to make the most of each moment.

That's when God showed me that I needed to learn to be content where I was, right where He had put me. I couldn't put everything on hold while I waited for Him to answer my prayer. I needed to learn to live each moment. That hasn't always been easy. For sure there are days when I daydream about the future with children.

But the process has been rewarding. Being content with where I am has reduced my worries and obsessions and ultimately allowed me to more intentionally enjoy the blessings God has given me.

My husband and I got married in 2001. I know many couples who had children early in their marriage and never truly got to know each other. When storms came, their marriages took a beating—and in some cases, those marriages didn't survive. While my husband and I both look forward to a day when God blesses us with children, we have taken the opportunity to live as a family of two and develop our relationship and enjoy our time as husband and wife. I often jokingly describe us as "that couple" who does everything together, but the reality is that we do exactly that. God has blessed us with a rock-solid relationship that has been tested again and again through this journey. And we've come out stronger than ever.

Being content with where I am has also allowed me to focus on being successful in my job. Leadership opportunities have opened up for me as a result of allowing myself to be an influence in the lives of the people I work with. This has ultimately given me opportunities to show God's love to others in a way I may not have been able to do otherwise.

Along the way, we have had the opportunity to learn lessons from the parenting successes and failures of friends and family. This will ultimately make us better parents when God does answer our prayer.

This journey certainly wasn't my plan. But to find contentment I focus on what I have, not what I don't have. In doing so, I see that God has truly blessed me.

Contentment can be defined as a state of being satisfied with one's situation. This contentment comes *despite* one's circumstances, not *because of* those circumstances.

I'm not happy that I suffer from infertility. I'm not joyful in my disappointment. But God has taught me to be content in my journey.

Ninth Installment

PATIENCE

> *Be still before the Lord and*
> *wait patiently for him...*
> (Psalm 37:7)

WAITING IS THE hardest part. I'm not a particularly patient person. I'm probably about average. Like most people, I don't like long lines in stores or red traffic lights... but they're part of life. So I turn on the radio or distract myself by watching the people around me. And eventually my turn comes.

As a child, I remember that my sister and I would stay up late into the night in anxious anticipation of Christmas morning, almost beside ourselves with excitement. But the night would seem to last forever.

Then, all of a sudden, it was Christmas morning.

My waiting has been a lot longer than just one night or a few traffic lights. I've discovered that it's one thing to say God is in control and knows what He is doing, and something altogether different to exercise patience and wait for it to happen.

I am thirteen years into this journey. I have planned and replanned and replanned again, more times than I can count. Anyone who has been through infertility will tell you that they work out the important dates every month and figure out how they'll coincide with events in your life. "If I get pregnant now, I can tell my family when I see them at Christmas" or "If I get pregnant now, my son/daughter will be the same age as his/her cousins" or "If I get pregnant now, my friend and I will be pregnant at the same time."

When Deon and I started trying to have a baby, our timing coincided perfectly with another couple we had befriended. We planned to start our new families together. We would go on maternity leave together and our children would play together. We would support each other as our children grew up together. It was a great plan and we were very excited.

Our friends now have two children, ages nine and seven, and they make a beautiful little family. I love their kids and am so happy for them.

But one of the hardest days of this journey came when she first told me that she was pregnant. My plan had made so much sense, so why wasn't God's plan the same?

The word patience can be defined as "the ability to wait for a long time without becoming annoyed or upset."[3] If I truly examine my behaviour over the years, I don't think that I have managed that. I have waited, not that I have much choice, but I do so a bit like an impatient child who stamps her feet every so often and screams "Why can't I have my way?"

Every couple of months, it seems that I reach my breaking point and find myself annoyed or upset. Mostly it's in the privacy of my prayer closet where I call out to God and ask Him why. "Why do I have to wait so long? Why does it hurt so bad? Why can everyone else get pregnant but I can't?"

---

[3] "Patience," *Britannica Dictionary*. Date of access: February 3, 2025 (https://www.britannica.com/dictionary/patience).

Occasionally Deon is in the wrong place at the wrong time and gets to see me fall apart. I cry, sob, then pick up and start going again.

They say that patience is a virtue, but I think it's strange that some people have it naturally and others have to work very hard at it.

Some people, like my dad, seem to have tons of patience. He was a music teacher who taught twenty to thirty often badly behaved students at a time how to play loud, sometimes obnoxious band instruments. While that can be stressful and very trying, he didn't often get annoyed or upset.

Other people in my life, and I won't mention names, have no patience at all. They get upset over small inconveniences and minor mistakes.

I think that patience can only be learned by being forced to wait for long periods of time. If we never had to wait, how would we learn to have patience?

I've always considered myself to be a reasonably patient person, but this journey has been teaching me that I still have a long way to go.

As I look back though, I can see just how far God has brought me. The much younger version of myself who first started trying to conceive was devastated every month. If you had told me then that I would have to wait at least thirteen years, I don't think I could have kept on the journey.

The older, more patient version of myself can now accept that I've waited this long. Since it didn't kill me, I know that I can continue to wait.

God has brought me this far. He'll see me through to the end.

Tenth Installment

THE ANCHOR HOLDS

*… we who have fled to take hold of the hope set
before us may be greatly encouraged. We have
this hope as an anchor for the soul…*
(Hebrews 6:18–19)

ON OCTOBER 15, 2014, eight years and exactly two months after Deon and I first began trying to conceive, I found out that I was pregnant.

I had suspected I might be pregnant for about a week but forced myself to wait for Saturday morning to take the pregnancy test. I was so excited that I didn't sleep well the night before. By 5:30 a.m., I was wide awake in bed, waiting. Deon was also awake; but while I was excited, he was afraid that we would yet again be disappointed.

Finally, I gave up the fight and went to "pee on a stick."

Staring at the little + sign on the pregnancy test felt surreal. Finally I was pregnant… and I had no clue how to feel or how to react.

I took the pregnancy test with me and went back to bed. I turned on the lamp and announced to Deon, "We're having a baby!"

Since Deon needs glasses and can't see well without them, and since he didn't have them in bed with him, it took a while to convince him. We then spent the next few hours laughing and crying and staring at the little "+" sign that would change our lives.

Finally it had happened. The wait had been worth it. We were going to become parents. God had answered our prayers and fulfilled His promise to me.

Words cannot adequately express the joy we felt or the relief that came from me no longer wondering whether I would ever be a mother. Deon and I spent the next couple of months, like all parents-to-be, revelling in the excitement of the new addition, telling immediate family and close friends, and thinking about baby names. We thanked God daily and gave Him praise for our little miracle.

We bought the books, the rocking chair, and the cutest little pair of reindeer booties. We even took pictures with the booties and had Christmas cards made to send to all our friends and extended family. The timing was perfect, as we would hit the twelve-week mark on December 15 and could tell everyone in time for Christmas.

On December 11, we went to the low-risk maternity clinic for our first appointment. It was so exciting. We would get to hear the baby's heartbeat.

We met the nurse and doctor and went through all the first-time pregnancy questions and answers. Then the doctor pulled out the machine to listen to the heartbeat.

She couldn't find one.

"Don't worry," she said. "We'll send you for an ultrasound, as their equipment is better."

Deon suspected the worst. I stayed positive, or maybe I was just in denial.

That afternoon, I waited in the ultrasound room to hear a heartbeat that never came. Our baby died at nine weeks along.

The emotional wave hit like a tsunami. My world was sucked out from under me and I stood still, looking around and wondering what on earth had happened. Then, with crushing force, the storm broke and I was pulled into the swirling waters of grief.

I cannot describe that period of time. The only analogy I can think to use is that I was swept away.

Deon and I ran. We dropped everything, took time off work, cancelled our plans for Christmas parties, and left town. We went to our cottage and hid. No visitors, no phone calls, no email. We told everyone via text message so we wouldn't need to talk to anyone.

The next week could only be described as the most difficult time of my life. My body hadn't realized that the baby had died, so I continued to feel pregnancy symptoms. I required medical assistance to force my body to clean itself out. Physically, it was the most intense pain I ever experienced. Emotionally, it was devastating. Spiritually, I fell apart.

How could this have happened? I'd been given a promise from God. How could He have let this happen? How could He be so cruel?

I would like to say that I clung to my faith in God and rested in His peace and comfort. The truth is that I was angry. I guess a good psychologist would say that being angry is a normal part of grieving—but I had never been this angry before, and certainly not at God. I had been raised in the church and lived all my life there. I wasn't even sure I was *allowed* to be this angry at God.

Physically, I healed rather quickly. Spiritually and emotionally, it took a little longer.

I didn't know how to deal with the emotions and questions swirling in my mind, so I just put one foot in front of the other, day after day. I felt numb.

I went to church but couldn't bring myself to sing about God's love and faithfulness. I went to work but didn't enter into any personal conversations with coworkers. I spent time with friends but didn't allow the conversation to get too personal or deep. I was on autopilot.

About a month later, as I sat in church, finally able to sing the songs and listen to the sermon without crying my eyes out, a revelation dawned on me.

I had been tossed into the stormy sea of grief. I didn't know which way was up. I was washed out to sea and lost. My boat was drifting...

But then I felt a tug. My anchor had caught in the cleft of the Rock.

Eleventh Installment
OBEDIENCE

*Does the Lord delight in burnt offerings and sac-
rifices as much as in obeying the Lord? To obey
is better than sacrifice, and to heed is better
than the fat of rams.*
(1 Samuel 15:22)

A LONG TIME ago, God laid on my heart the desire to start writing down these lessons. It has taken more than a decade, numerous stops and starts, and a lot of prompts from God to see this book finished.

If I'm honest with you, and with myself, I've been disobedient in not getting this done sooner. Time after time, God has spoken to me through sermons and songs. That still, small voice has told me to write this book. I don't know why. I don't even know what I'll do with this book when it's finished… but still I get reminded again and again.

Similar to a parent who doesn't reward a disobedient child with a gift, I believe God is telling me to complete this book before I'm blessed with a child. This isn't because God is spiteful, but because He knows the bigger picture—and in that bigger picture, I need to have done this for some reason. This is similar to the parent who tells their child to do his homework. When the child then asks to go out and play, the parent asks whether he has done his homework. The parent won't let him have his request approved until he has done what he was supposed to do.

God has called us to be obedient regardless of where we are in our journey. He is who He is no matter where I am and He requires obedience. It's interesting to me that this is one of the last lessons He has shown me. Learning to trust Him was a prerequisite to learning to obey Him. I can now see that obedience comes out of trust.

The truth is that although writing these lessons down is in some ways cathartic, it is also very painful. God has been using this process to release the pain and help me move on. But in doing so, I am required to relive each of these installments again and again.

My response to infertility may be unique, but infertility itself is not. Infertility has been an affliction to women for thousands of years. From the beginning, in Genesis, the Bible tells us stories of Sarah, Rachel, Elizabeth, and many others who suffered in similar ways. What makes my journey unique to me is how I choose to respond to the experiences I go through.

As a part of this process, God has planted a seed in my heart about using my faith journey to help others who are facing similar paths. I heard that particular prompting from God in church one Sunday morning. I don't remember exactly when it happened, the specific topic of the sermon, or even who was speaking, but I do remember the scripture that was read: *"[He] comforts us in all our troubles, so that we can comfort those in any trouble with the comfort we ourselves receive from God"* (2 Corinthians 1:4).

I also remember the picture God gave me. In it, I was sharing my experience with other women suffering from infertility, using my book as a way to share in their pain and let them know that they're not alone. I don't know how that will happen, but I do know that it can't happen if I don't finish the book.

And so I keep working on it.

Last Installment
GOD ALWAYS KEEPS HIS PROMISES

Now to him who is able to do immeasurably
more than all we ask or imagine, according to
his power that is at work within us...
(Ephesians 3:20)

IF THIS WAS someone else's story and I was reading it for the first time, I would want to know that the story ends with a "happily ever after." Unfortunately, that ending has yet to be written. At the time of this writing, thirteen years after we first started trying to conceive, I still am not a mother.

I haven't written the final installment yet, but I know that it's coming! The Bible assures us that God always keeps His promises. So I'm taking all my other lessons to heart and waiting patiently—most of the way, at least—on God.

His plan is perfect, and for certain it's better than anything I could ever imagine, for He is a big God with big plans. His timing is perfect, too. I may not understand it, and I may not like it, but He knows best.

I am waiting on Him.

Epilogue
GOD IS FAITHFUL

I prayed for this child, and the Lord has granted
me what I asked of him.
(1 Samuel 1:27)

ONE NIGHT IN March 2021, I was feeling slightly nauseous and a little hopeful. I took a chance and took a pregnancy test.

I was rewarded with one of the most glorious and unbelievable sights: the word *pregnant*.

The emotions were overwhelming. We were shocked. We had been believing God for this, but to see it happen after so much time? It was a little hard to grasp. In fact, when I showed Deon the pregnancy test, it took him forty-five minutes to even acknowledge what I was showing him.

We were elated. After all this time, our prayers had been answered.

But at the same time, we tried desperately not to get our hopes up. After all, we had been here before and it hadn't ended well.

The first three months were perhaps some of the longest of my life. All this time, we kept waiting for that all-important first ultrasound when we would hear the baby's heartbeat. I was forty-three years old, so it was considered a high-risk pregnancy.

But this time around it felt different. I was experiencing every pregnancy symptom imaginable. And while I was pretty miserable, I was also rejoicing in each and every symptom.

The day finally came for us to go for the twelve-week ultrasound. Deon and I were extremely anxious as we walked into the ultrasound clinic, but it only took a moment on the examination table for us to hear that heartbeat. Our tears flowed freely. It was a healthy, bouncing baby.

It was a miracle.

Once we passed that milestone, we relaxed into the rest of the pregnancy and allowed our hope for the future to blossom in our hearts, and in my belly. We were awed again and again by the miracle of pregnancy that allows a mother's body to change, flex, accommodate, and support the baby growing inside. The creation of a child, from conception through birth and beyond, is so complex and precise… yet it all happened exactly as it should. God was surely at work!

It should never have happened. The facts tell the story: I was forty-three years old—not ancient, perhaps, but certainly beyond the expected childbearing years. The probability of conception is extremely low at that age. We had been married for twenty years and actively trying to conceive for fifteen, so our likelihood of success had been very low.

But God is a God of miracles and He is faithful to keep the promises He has made to His children.

And so one day in November 2021, exactly twenty-five years after Deon and I went on our first date, the doctors placed an eight-pound, three-ounce miracle in our arms.

We called her McKayla Joy.

And every night we sing to her those beautiful words: "Jesus loves you, this I know…"

www.ingramcontent.com/pod-product-compliance
Lightning Source LLC
Chambersburg PA
CBHW071457070426
42452CB00040B/1557